GW00706169

The Little Book of
GREAT
Aussie
Slang

Edited by Sonya Plowman

The Five Mile Press

INTRODUCTION

We all do it – use slang that is.
Whether you belong to the cafe
latte set or are more at home
sinking a cold one at the local,
you're bound to use our
colourful Aussie slang in
everyday conversation. And now
the next time you chew the fat
with a mate, you'll know exactly
what they mean when they tell
you they've got to be off like a
bride's nightie. Bloody oath!

Sonya Plowman

a bit rich
cheeky; over the top.

above board
legal; out in the open.

accident
an unplanned pregnancy.

air between the ears
to be slow, unintelligent.

all systems go
all is ready.

ancient history
facts that are now old news, no
longer important.

Anne's your aunty
expression indicating all is fine.

any
sex, e.g. did she give you any?

a over t
arse over tit; falling over in a
very undignified way.

Aussie salute
the flapping away of ever-
present flies from one's face.

'ave a go, ya mug!
cricket fan's taunt (to a slow batsman).

back o' Bourke
any remote, isolated place.

backwater
an unsophisticated, remote
place.

backy
tobacco.

backyard job
illegal; improper;
done without
red tape.

bad trot
run of bad luck.

ball and chain
wife.

banana bender
Queenslander.

bang in the middle
dead centre.

barney
fight.

bash
wild party.

beef
complaint; to complain.

bender
a drinking binge.

bend the elbow
drink excessively.

bingle
a minor car accident.

Black Stump
a non-existent place in the
middle of nowhere.

blahdy blah blah
etcetera; all the rest.

blanky
euphemistic term for bloody.

blind
very drunk.

13

blow through
depart hastily.

boink
to have sexual intercourse.

botch
to mess up something, e.g. he
botched it up.

brassed off
really annoyed or angry.

brick short of a wall
simple person.

Buckley's
next to no chance, e.g. you've
got Buckley's of getting the job.

bug out
depart, e.g. let's bug out of here.

bung on
to put on, especially in relation
to food. e.g. to bung on a snag.

burl
an attempt, e.g. give it a burl.

bushed
exhausted.

cactus
dead; broken; ruined.

cahoots
(in...with) in partnership with,
often suggesting illegality.

call Ralph
to vomit.

Ralph!

camp as a row of tents
said of a homosexual male.

can't handle
to dislike or be unwilling to
accept.

chamber of horrors
a disgusting or horrific place.

charming!
said to display one's disgust or
disapproval.

checkout chick
cash-register operator.

chew the fat
chat.

chickenfeed
a meagre amount of money.

choked up
overwhelmed with emotion.

Christmas on a stick
something special, e.g. what do
you think you are, Christmas on
a stick?

chuck a wobbly
throw a temper tantrum.

chuck it in
give up; quit.

chunder
vomit.

clever-dick
conceited, know-it-all person.

clinging vine
emotionally dependent person.

clockwatcher
person who constantly checks
the time, e.g. those in boring
jobs.

come a clanger
make an embarrassing mistake.

cop a feel
to touch someone
sexually, usually
of a man to a
woman.

cossie
swimming
costume.

cossie

couldn't fart in a bottle
utterly useless.

couldn't lie straight in bed
of a compulsive cheat or liar.

couldn't organise a fart in a
bean factory
stupid.

couple of pies short of a
grand final
stupid.

cow of a thing
anything frustrating or
infuriating.

crapper
toilet.

creamed
beaten soundly, particularly in a
sporting match.

cushy
well paid, undemanding job.

cuts me up
makes me laugh.

cut the crap
stop talking rubbish.

cut up
extremely upset.

dab hand at
skilled; good at.

daks
trousers.

dead cert
a sure thing; a certainty,
especially pertaining to horse-
racing.

dead horse
tomato sauce.

delish
delicious.

dero
a derelict; a vagrant; a homeless
alcoholic.

desperate
wanting sex so badly that one
would go out with someone very
ugly in order to do it.

died in the arse
failed miserably.

divvy van
police van.

dog's breakfast
a huge mess.

don't strain yourself!
said to someone who's not
helping with the task at hand.

dosh
money.

down to the last crust
dead broke.

do your nut
throw a tantrum.

dreaded lurgy
an infectious illness; usually the
cold or flu.

drill
procedure, e.g. what's the drill?

drop-kick
an idiot.

drop (one's) lunch
to fart.

Dutch oven
act of farting under the
blankets.

earbasher
boring person who talks
incessantly.

easy lay
a woman who is easy to have
sex with.

el cheapo
anything that is of inferior
quality; not manufactured well.

every bastard and his dog
everyone.

everything's rosy
all is going well.

exchange notes
to gossip.

eye off
to stare at, often with intent to
steal.

eyes like roadmaps
bloodshot, red eyes.

fair crack of the whip
request for fair treatment.

fallen woman
a woman with a ruined
reputation.

falsies
fake eyelashes or breasts; false
teeth.

fandangled thing
frustrating contraption that is
hard to operate.

fantasamagorical
wonderful; amazing.

feel crook
feel unwell.

fell off the back of the truck
pertaining to something that
has been stolen.

fight dirty
to use unfair tactics.

flak
an onslaught of criticism.

flake out
to collapse from exhaustion.

flat chat
very fast; very busy.

flibbertigibbet
gossiping, talkative girl.

floater
faeces that refuse to be flushed
down the toilet.

flog a dead horse
to continue trying something
when it obviously won't work.

floozie
promiscuous female.

fly a kite
a rude way of saying 'go away'.

fob off
to treat someone rudely; to
virtually ignore them.

foggiest
no idea or clue. e.g. I haven't
got the foggiest.

for the sake of Mary!
said when annoyed or
exasperated.

frig around
to mess around; behave stupidly.

from a mile off
very obvious.

*full as a fat woman's
underwear*
drunk.

full of it
someone who talks nonsense; a
conceited person.

gadabout
socially active person.

game's up
when someone is caught in the
act of an illicit activity.

get a dose
contract a venereal disease.

get a leg in the door
make progress.

get a load
have a look, e.g. get a load of
what she's wearing!

get a wriggle on
hurry up.

get the arse
get fired from work.

get the drift
understand; comprehend.

get the nod
gain approval to go ahead with a
plan.

get the rough end of the pineapple
get worse treatment than others in a given situation.

give someone the irrits
annoy; irritate someone.

give someone the rounds of the kitchen
give someone a severe telling-off.

give someone the willies
make someone's skin crawl; create tension, uneasiness.

go down like a lead balloon
to be received badly. e.g. that
joke you told went down like a
lead balloon.

go for a burn
drive fast; test-drive a car.

*going to see a man about a
dog*
to urinate; to go somewhere
without revealing exactly
where.

go like hot cakes
sell easily and quickly.

go like the clappers
go very fast.

good get
in sport, a good catch or
retrieval of the ball.

go off half-cocked
to rush into something without
thinking.

Gordon Bennett!
exclamation of exasperation or
surprise.

got me
I don't know.

*got space to rent between
the ears*
brainless.

grab by the balls
to render someone under one's
control.

ground-splasher
said of person urinating in
public.

gun it
go fast, particularly in a car.

guy thing
something that only men
understand or want to do.

hack
careless, incompetent person.

had it soft
to have had a carefree, easy time.

half-baked
incomplete; not fully formed.

half-pint
short person.

hanger-on
a person who clings to others; a
freeloader.

hang out for
wait with much anticipation.

hang the expense!
never mind what it costs!

happy as Larry
extremely happy.

hasn't got a brass razzo
penniless.

have a burl
give it a go; try it.

hell for leather
very fast.

hinges on
all depends on.

hit-and-giggle
social game of tennis, usually
involving women.

holus-bolus
all of it; all at once.

holy guacamole!
expression of surprise or
wonderment.

hoodwinked
cheated; tricked.

how's it hanging?
how is everything going?

howya goin' mate, orright?
popular greeting between males.

humdinger
really good person, thing or
event.

hurl
to vomit.

if it was raining custard I'd only have a fork
to be very unlucky.

I'll pay that
acknowledgement that one has been outsmarted.

is it a goer?
is it going to happen; does it work?

it's a take
the situation is a deception or
fraud.

it's just not cricket
not the right thing to do; not
fair; against protocol.

*I've seen better heads on a
glass of beer*
insult about someone ugly.

jerkin' the gherkin
to masturbate; to delude
oneself.

jiminy cricket!
an exclamation of wonder or
surprise.

just quietly
just between you and me.

keen as mustard
very enthusiastic.

keep it all in the family
keep discussions/secrets within
a group to the exclusion of
others.

keep (one's) pecker up
keep cheerful, despite goings-
on.

keep your shirt on!
settle down; don't lose your
temper.

kettle of fish
problem; difficult situation.

knuckle sandwich
punch in the mouth.

kosher
genuine; the real thing.

Khyber Pass
arse

Lady Muck
arrogant woman who puts on
airs and graces.

leg opener
alcohol.

let 'er rip
enthusiastic command to start.

lickety spit
a quick wash.

*like a pickpocket at a
nudists' camp*
uncomfortable, out of place.

like a shag on a rock
alone; out of place.

like buggery
with great energy.

like the clappers
very fast.

little vegemites
children.

Can I have a sandwich mum?

loads
plenty of.

lob on over
come over; go over.

looker
very attractive person.

looks like the wild man from Borneo
a man of very untidy or neglected appearance.

lord it over (someone)
gloat about; domineer.

lost me
incomprehension of what is being said.

mad as a cut snake
insane; crazy.

*make a production of
(something)*
be a drama queen; over-fussy.

*make custard out of
(someone)*
to beat someone, either in a
fight or contest.

make it snappy
hurry up.

make like a tree and leave
go; get lost.

make mince-meat out of
to physically or verbally attack
someone.

malarky
rubbish; nonsense.

malley root
prostitute.

marching orders
to be sacked; to be thrown out
of a relationship.

marriage material
said of a person who would be
suitable to marry.

mate's rates
reduced rates for friends.

N

narniebar
banana.

no great shakes
nothing particularly
outstanding.

no object
no problem; of no importance.

no room to swing a cat
in relation to tiny, cramped
quarters.

nosh-up
a big meal.

not a bad old stick
a nice person.

not a patch on
nowhere near as good as.

not fussed
not worried; not particular
about which alternative is
chosen.

not give a hang
not worry about it, don't care.

not much chop
not very good; below
expectations.

not on your nellie
no way!

not the full packet of bickies
simple-minded; stupid.

not within cooee
not within hearing distance.

no wucking furries!
euphemism for 'no f***ing
worries'.

nudge the bottle
to drink excessive alcohol.

ocker
Australian; particularly
referring to uncouth,
chauvinistic males.

off like a bride's nightie
depart hastily.

off like a bucket of prawns
depart hastily.

off (one's) trolley
insane; irrational; mad.

oil
advice or information, e.g. give
me the oil on the merger.

okey dokey
good; okay, I'll do that.

old codger
old man.

old one-two
act of violence.

on a high
in a state of happiness.

on a sticky wicket
in trouble.

on the blink
not working.

on the bones of (one's) bum
destitute; financially ruined.

on the receiving end
to be the recipient of something
unpleasant.

on the turps
to describe someone drinking
alcohol to excess.

open-and-shut case
obvious; clear-cut.

out cold
unconscious.

out of circulation
socially recluse.

out of whack
disorderly; chaotic.

over a barrel
at a disadvantage.

packing polenta
to be extremely scared.

pack of bludgers
remark used to show contempt
for others.

paralytic
extremely drunk.

pavement pizza
vomit.

pearler
indicates excellence, e.g. she hit a pearler on the field today.

play funny buggers
behave stupidly; to cheat; be deceitful.

plonk
cheap wine.

pokie
poker machine.

preggers
pregnant.

presactly
combination of precisely and
exactly.

prolaby
probably.

prolly
shortened form of probably.

*put that in your pipe and
smoke it!*
a gloating insult to someone.

put the bite on
to ask for a loan.

queen it up
behaving like a homosexual.

quick as a wombat on a lazy day
dim-witted person.

quit harping
stop nagging.

rank and file
ordinary people; general
population.

rapt
overjoyed.

rare as rocking-horse shit
very uncommon.

rat-shit
no good; of very poor quality.

ready as a drover's dog
sexually aroused.

ready to drop
heavily pregnant.

rearrange someone's face
beat someone up.

receive the order of the boot
to get fired.

rego
vehicle registration.

rellies
relatives.

Richard Cranium
dickhead.

rooted
ruined; exhausted.

***run on the smell of an oily
rag***
very efficient; requiring a
minimum of fuel.

S

sanger
sandwich

seen better heads on a glass of beer
said of an ugly person.

see your last gumtree
die.

shack up with
live with (intimately).

shaggin' wagon
panel van or similar.

shaping up a beaut
coming along nicely.

shebang
affair; business.

shellacking
a physical or verbal beating.

shit a brick!
exclamation of surprise.

short and curlies
pubic hair.

short of numbers in the
Upper House
stupid.

shut your trap
be quiet!

sink a few
to drink beer.

sink the sausage
have sexual intercourse.

skedaddle
leave quickly.

splash the boots
urinate.

strapped (for cash)
short of money.

suss out
to find out; to get the required
information.

sweet!
exclamation of approval; that's
great!

sweet Fanny Adams
zilch; nothing; none.

T

the sticks
out in the country.

tired and emotional
drunk.

tough titties!
bad luck!

trouble and strife
wife.

two-pot screamer
one who gets drunk easily, and
in a less than dignified manner.

Uncle Chester
child molester.

*under the affluence of
inkahol*
drunk.

*up shit creek with only a
fork to paddle with*
in serious trouble.

Don't be vulgar!

up the duff
pregnant.

vague out
to stop paying attention.

vee-dub
Volkswagen.

village bike
promiscuous woman.

wake up Australia!
said to daydreamer.

walking papers
dismissal from work; the sack.

way gone
very drunk.

well turned out
dressed well.

westie
a person from the western suburbs (of Melbourne or Sydney).

what a wanker!
what a stupid, arrogant person!

what gives?
what is the explanation?

what's the damage?
how much do I owe?

what's the John Dory?
what's the story; what is happening?

who's your daddy?
used as a taunt or insult.

with me?
do you understand?

would bet on two flies
walking up the wall
of a compulsive gambler.

wouldn't know his arse from
his elbow
idiotic.

yahoo
lout; uncouth male.

yakka
physical labour.

yank
an American.

yobbo
lout; uncouth male.

yodel
to vomit.

you der!
you idiot!

youse
plural of you.

yowie
mythical Australian monster.

Z

zine
small, independent magazine,
generally focusing on a
particular theme.

The Five Mile Press

The Five Mile Press Pty Ltd
950 Stud Road, Rowville
Victoria 3178 Australia
Phone: +61 3 8756 5500
Email: publishing@fivemile.com.au

First published 2000
Reprinted 2001, 2002, 2003, 2004

Editor: Sonya Plowman
Cover design & illustrations: Geoff Hocking
Internal design: SBR Productions

Printed in China

National Library of Australia Cataloguing-in-Publication data
Great Aussie Slang
ISBN 1 86503 334 0

1. English language - Australia - Slang - Dictionaries.
2. Australianisms - Dictionaries. I. Plowman, Sonya.
427.994